Designed by Flowerpot Press in Franklin, TN.
www.FlowerpotPress.com
Designer: Jonas Fearon Bell
Editor: Johannah Gilman Paiva
PAB-0808-0119
ISBN: 978-1-4867-0555-9
Made in China/Fabriqué en Chine

Why Do Camels

Jennifer Shand

Illustrated by
T. G. Tjornehoj

Have Long Eyelashes?

How do animals survive in the desert? The desert is so hot and dry, with so little food, each desert animal must have something very special about them to help them live there.

Why do KANGAROOS HOP all of the time?

Is it because they are playing HOPSCOTCH
with their friends?

No, that's silly!

Kangaroos hop because it is the fastest
way to move around in the desert,
where they have to travel very
far to find food and water.

Why do CAMELS have LONG eyelashes?

Is it because they were PLAYING with their
mother's MAKE-UP?

No, that's silly!

Camels have long eyelashes because it keeps
the sand that is blowing around out of their eyes!

Why do ELEPHANTS have such BIG ears?

Is it so they can wear big EARRINGS?

No, that's silly!

Elephants have big ears because they act like
fans to help cool the elephant down in the
extreme heat of the desert.

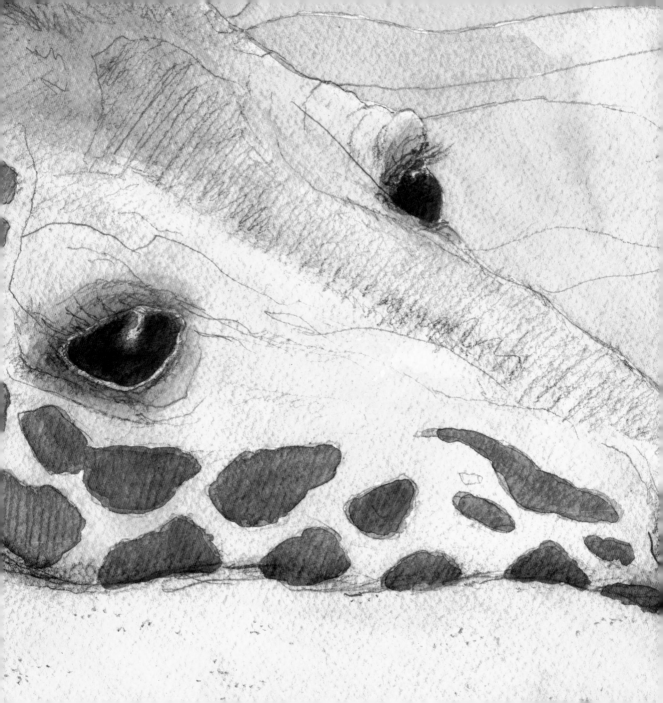

Why do GIRAFFES have BLUE tongues?

Is it because they have been
    LICKING a blue LOLLIPOP?

No, that's silly!

Giraffes have blue
tongues because their
tongues are in the sun
a lot while they are eating.
The blue acts like a
sunscreen so their
tongues will not
get burned!

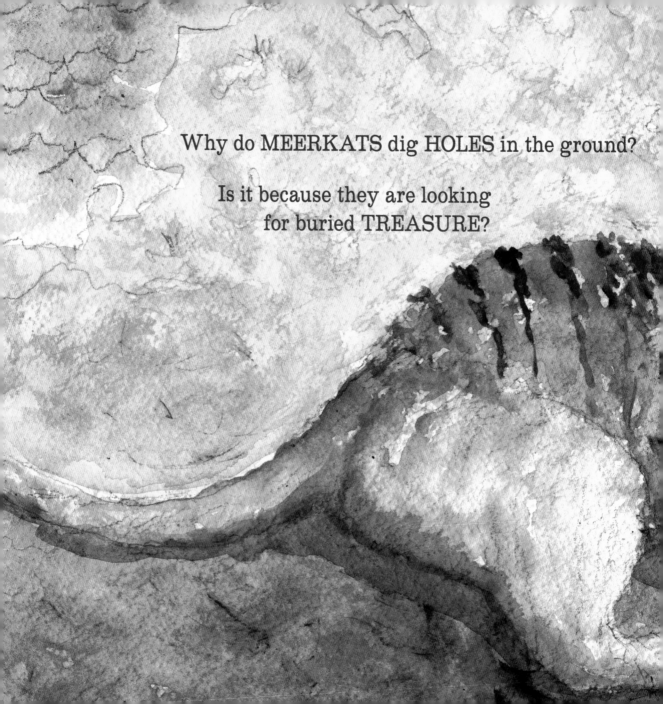

Why do MEERKATS dig HOLES in the ground?

Is it because they are looking
for buried TREASURE?

No, that's silly!

Meerkats dig holes to find food and build their underground homes. They live underground to get out of the heat of the sun during the day and they snuggle together during the night to stay warm.